THIS little LIGHT
OF MINE

*This Little Light of Mine*

JENÉ SAIS QUOI

Copyright © Jené Sais Quoi

All rights reserved. No part of this publication may be reproduced, distributed, or transmitted in any form or by any means, including photocopying, recording, or other electronic or mechanical methods, without the prior written permission of the publisher, except in the case of brief quotations embodied in critical reviews and certain other non-commercial uses permitted by copyright law. For permission requests, write to the publisher, addressed "Attention: Permissions Coordinator," at the address below.

ISBN: 979-8-218-45969-7 (Hardcover)

Library of Congress Control Number: 2024912805

Any references to historical events, real people, or real places are used fictitiously. Names, characters, and places are products of the author's imagination.
Front cover image by Y Hanson / JSQ Productions

Book Cover design by Pandora Designs

First printing edition 2025.

INDASHIO INK. 767 Broadway #1413 New York, NY, 10003

www.jsqworld.com

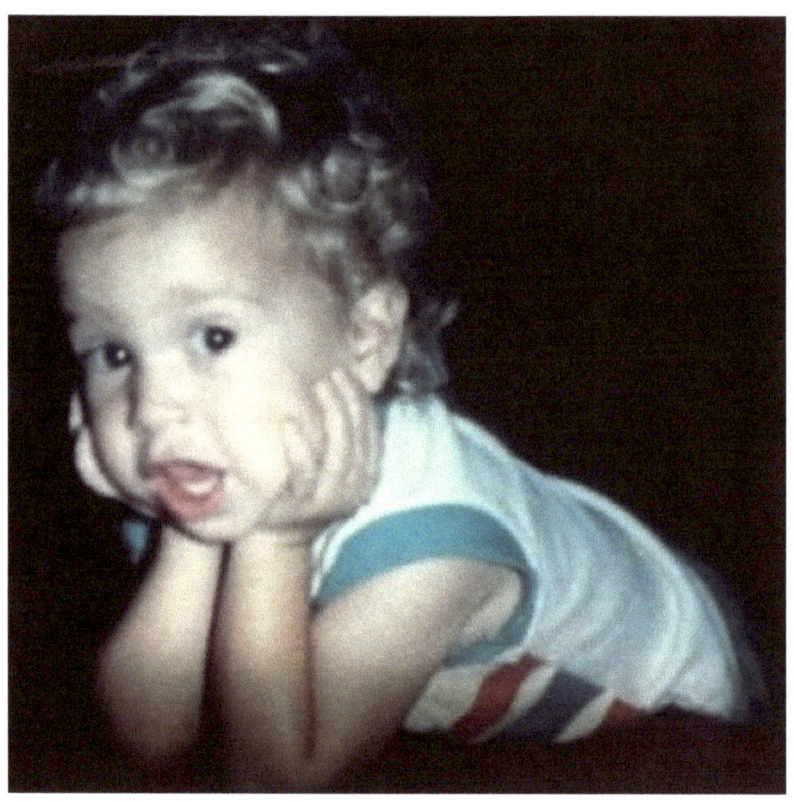

This book is dedicated to the little girl who was kept in the dark for so long who wasn't able to shine her bright light and got lost in the darkness. It is now her time to shine!

I also want to dedicate this book to all the people, friends, family, and supporters my Tin Mans, Scarecrows and Lions I met on this journey. Thank you! Thank you for your love, support, encouragement. To my parents who are the definition of unconditional love.

# CONTENTS

| | |
|---|---|
| **PROLOGUE** | 7 |
| **1. BEING BRAD** | 11 |
| **2. BECOMING INDASHIO** | 27 |
| **3. END OF AN ERA** | 59 |
| **4. BECOMING JENÉ** | 77 |

# PROLOGUE

Eva and I settled next to each other on the couch, a bowl of popcorn between us, ready to watch an episode of the TV show "Transparent." It was one of the first major shows to feature an openly transgender character. I saw so much of myself in the main character, Maura; but unlike Maura, I hadn't yet found the courage to name who I truly was.

At that time, I was in the depths of a personal purgatory. Just a few years before, I'd been at the pinnacle of my career as a fashion designer; I'd won a nationally televised design competition and been featured in major magazines. I'd done countless celebrity cover and fashion shoots with the likes of Kim Kardashian. I'd had a penthouse apartment with a hot tub in the living room with my name on it. Now I was crashing on my friend Eva's couch; her friendship was the only thing standing between me and homelessness. I was broke. I hadn't even been able to buy Christmas presents for my family that year. The fashion career I'd worked so hard to build was now precarious at best.

But worst of all, I'd become unrecognizable to myself. Deeply unhappy despite my acquaintance with fame and success, I'd managed to alienate many of my closest allies. I'd lost my ability to sustain the fragile alter ego I'd constructed for myself as a bulwark against a world where I'd never belonged. I knew that that alter ego, "Indashio," was dying—but I didn't know who else I was allowed to be. I felt like a shell of a person; the lights were on, but nobody was home.

As the episode unfolded before us onscreen, I began to feel a sense of recognition. Watching Jeffrey Tambor's character, Maura, take pride in carefully adorning herself, I thought of the nights I'd dressed in my apartment for no one but myself: feeling the fabric drape around my shoulders, seeing my body held by the soft lines of the dress, I'd known that this was who I really was. But I hadn't yet had the confidence to go out in the world dressed like this. In these moments, I thought of myself as inhabiting a character in drag; I called her "Courtney."

Then the story flashed back to a scene in Maura's childhood. As a child, Maura is always out of place; the girls don't want her, but she isn't interested in hanging out with the boys. When she tries on her sister's dress, her mother admonishes her that dresses are for girls.

I felt my eyes brimming with tears: this was my story. I had been that girl. I suddenly understood, with heartbreaking clarity, that that girl was the real me, and that I had to do right by her. I had to figure out how to honor her by being myself.

When the episode ended, Eva turned and looked at me

softly. She could see how the episode had affected me. "Do you think," she asked gently, "that you might be trans?"

"Yes," I replied, quietly but with no hesitation. "I think I am."

This book is dedicated to that young girl, and to all the others out there like her. I've always had a fierce inner light that wanted to shine upon the world—I believe we all do. But the world does not always know how to receive our light. I spent decades shapeshifting and adapting: building alter egos, finding ways to mold my persona so that I'd make sense to the world around me. Now I finally make sense to myself, and I'm ready to tell my story.

# 1

## BEING BRAD

### Boys Don't Wear Dresses

I was born on January 16, 1984, in Pittsfield, Massachusetts. My parents had both grown up in the area; both from large, working class families (my dad was one of six, my mom one of eight), they'd met at a local carnival. They married young and had me soon after. My sister, whom I'll call "Angel," would follow two years later, and my other sister "Mary" when I was eight years old.

Now, I look with both sadness and compassion on my young parents, who must have been thrilled to have a son—or, more accurately, to think they had a son. They'd grown up with certain ideas of what that meant, and it was only natural that they'd project those ideas onto me. My dad had never had a father himself; growing up, his mother had a string of relationships with abusive men. Perhaps he thought that, with his own son, he'd have a chance to get it right. He must have been ecstatic at the thought of a son to go fishing with, or whose basketball games he might coach to victory. Especially at the time, no one expected to have a gay or trans child. Thankfully, cultural expectations and norms are now changing—but not for everyone.

I like to say that I came out with my tippy-toes pointed, ready for the stage. Looking back, I can see that I always knew who I was, and was ready to show the world—though the world wasn't always ready for me.

My first memory of being told "no" is when I was about four years old. My mother caught me trying on one of my sister's dresses; I loved my sister's wardrobe, especially her Cinderella gown. I still remember the shocked look on my mother's face. "Take that off," she said. "Boys don't wear dresses." It was my first memory of shame. I felt like something was wrong with me—like I didn't understand the rules everyone else seemed to effortlessly intuit.

That experience taught me not to wear dresses in front of other people, but it didn't change the way I saw myself. When my parents weren't looking, I would wrap a blanket around my waist and pretend it was a dress. I'd lock myself in the bathroom and pull my T-shirt around my head so that it looked like long hair. I could have stayed in there for hours, gazing at the girl in the mirror.

I never gave up my obsession with Cinderella. I drew countless pictures of her in her ball gown. Our house had a fireplace, and sometimes I'd play in the ashes, imagining my parents as the wicked stepmother forcing me to clean the house while my sisters went to the ball. In this persona, I'd sometimes talk back to my parents—"Don't tell me what to do!" (My Cinderella was hostile and sassy, not timid like the Disney version). My parents might be able to control what I wore in public, but they couldn't control my imagination.

In Kindergarten, I kissed my first boy, on the playground. The reaction from my teachers was swift and clear: "You're not allowed to kiss boys." I took the deeper lesson to heart, though the reasons behind it weren't clear: because I was a boy, it was wrong to like boys, or to let other boys like me. My feelings themselves, it turned out, could be wrong.

For Christmas one year, all I wanted was a Barbie Dream House. My grandma thought it would be cute to have a male relative call the house as "Santa" and ask each of us what we wanted. When I excitedly whispered my wish into the phone, Santa paused and then replied, "You can't have that. How about a truck or something?" I hung up the phone and ran to my mom, crying; she later admonished my grandma, but the lesson stayed with me.

Another Christmas, instead of the Barbie I wanted, I got a fishing pole. I remember miserably watching as my sisters and girl cousins played with their dolls, brushing their hair and dressing them up, unable to participate in the games I so desperately wanted to play.

In other words, my family took pains early on to teach me what it meant to be Brad. There was a right way and a wrong way to be Brad, because there was a right way and a wrong way to be a boy.

After some time, I learned the lesson: there were certain taboos surrounding the body I was born into. But rather than muffling my inner light, I found a way to shapeshift, like a chameleon, and find ways to express myself.

For example: dresses might have been off the table, but there were other ways to indulge my love for fashion. I still remember writing the word "DESIGN"—one of the first words I learned to spell—and proudly showing it to my teacher. At age nine, I went through a phase of wearing full suits to school (my grandmother bought them for me at JC Penney). I completed the look with a trench coat, fedora, and even a briefcase.

As I moved through childhood, I tried to stay as true to myself as possible, but compromises and disappointments were inevitable. I remember going to a summer camp that was segregated by genders. I didn't want to wear swim trunks; I wanted a swimsuit like a girl's. In the end, my parents bought me a wrestling outfit, and I wore that into the lake.

I wanted to go in the girls' cabin with my sister and cousin, but of course I was shepherded into the boys' cabin. I had nothing in common with my cabin-mates: they were rough and cared mostly about sports, while I just wanted to do arts and crafts all day. One day, when the whole camp gathered in the morning, the counselors separated the boys and girls for an activity. "You can go on the girls' side," joked one of the counselors, gesturing at me; the entire camp laughed. I felt my face burning in shame. Not only was it obvious that I didn't belong—to them, my unbelonging was little more than a joke.

## This Little Light

Though being Brad meant hiding certain aspects of who I was, there were moments when I felt recognized.

Once, at a carnival with a cousin and her grandmother, we were waiting in line for the pony ride. "She can go next," said the attendant, gesturing toward me. The grandmother corrected him: "He's a boy!" But I couldn't stop smiling; I knew that, in that one moment, I had been seen for who I was.

I always loved performing. My favorite toy was my Star Stage; I'd sing "Do the Locomotion" into the microphone, holding my body in elegant poses, imagining the whole world watching me.

In fifth grade, I finally got my chance to perform for a real audience, singing "This Little Light of Mine" as a solo at school graduation. It was thrilling to be in the spotlight; I thought this is where I belong. Now, when I remember those lyrics, I think that song choice was particularly meaningful. I knew that I had an inner light meant to shine upon the world. Those around me might have been more comfortable if I hid it under a bushel—but I was going to find ways to let it shine.

Growing up in Pittsfield as a trans girl was like living in a fishbowl. I felt everyone's eyes on me, monitoring my appearance and behavior, taking note of when I departed from the script.

Thankfully, I always had a sense that there was more for me out there—that there was some Elsewhere where I'd make sense, a larger stage where I could fully inhabit myself and manifest my dreams.

In fifth grade, for a school project, my teacher had us research faraway places by writing to tourism boards and asking for brochures (this was, of course, the pre-Internet era, when printed matter offered the only portal to possible other worlds, and travel plans could not be made with the click of a button). Beguiled by the idea, I wrote to every place I could think of. Gleaming brochures began arriving in my mailbox, from Nebraska to Singapore. I'd pore over them endlessly, dreaming of escape.

I decided to become a travel agent. I'd always been intrigued by business; I loved branding logos and spent time learning about corporations. I was fascinated by cash registers and banks with safes. Perhaps, I thought, I could combine my business aspirations with my travel dreams, and make something happen.

I set up an office in the family basement, "hiring" a friend as my first employee. I called the places I wanted to visit, pretending to be a legitimate adult professional ("Hi, I'm calling from Around The World Travel…"). My first successful project was obtaining a trip to Disney World for my family. When I'd asked my parents to take us there before, they'd simply laughed and dismissed the idea: how could we possibly afford it? No one we knew took expensive vacations. So I took matters into my own hands. Wielding my self-bestowed authority as the head of my newly formed agency, I called Disney World and requested a commission for booking my family's trip—and, somewhat to my own surprise, was granted a substantial discount. When I presented the idea to my parents again—this time with hard numbers and evidence of the money I'd saved them—they had to shake their heads and acquiesce. We had the time of our lives on the trip, and after that my parents found a way to take us every year.

More than the trip itself, it was the confirmation of my own agency and power that made this experience a transformative one. I'd wanted to see what the world beyond Pittsfield had to offer, and I wouldn't take my parents' "no" for an answer. It was the first time I discovered my own ability to hustle—to ask for what I wanted and persuade others to give it to me. On a deeper level, I felt like I had manifested the trip: I'd committed unwaveringly to my inner vision, and in confidently taking steps in its direction, the universe had met me more than halfway. This was an important lesson, one that would serve me well in the next phase of my life. There was no need to stay stuck in the Bermuda Triangle of others' scripts and expectations: I could create my own reality.

## Not Adam and Steve

Erin, my travel agency "employee," once casually mentioned, "My grandma says that boys who play with dolls are gay, and that you're going to be gay when you grow up." I'd already learned that I couldn't be a girl; I wasn't totally sure what "gay" was, but I knew it was something you didn't want to be.

In the 80s and early 90s—the height of the AIDS crisis—the stigma against homosexuality was real. Phrases like "It's Adam and Eve, not Adam and Steve" abounded. Marriage equality was a distant dream, and gay people were blamed and scapegoated for their own deaths. The message was clear: "If you're gay, you're going to get AIDS, and probably also go to hell."

My own family reinforced many of these messages. I remember hearing members of my extended family bashing or making jokes about gay people. Once, on a family trip to Provincetown, my mom saw a lesbian couple holding hands; her face twisted up in disgust and she said, "Ew, gross."

In the cutthroat social environment of middle school, any vulnerability could result in shunning or actual violence. I knew that I had to avoid "seeming gay" at all costs. I shaved my head and tried to mold my speech and walk to resemble my peers. I hung out with a group of kids nobody messed with, hoping that would protect me. I didn't smoke, but I pretended I did, so as to fit in and avoid peer pressure. Once, my dad found a note a classmate had passed me, referring to "the smokes"; the note earned me a beating. There was no way I could explain the real situation without also revealing why I felt so vulnerable.

By eighth grade, I had a couple of girlfriends, trying as best I could to blend in with my heterosexual peers. I was petrified of touching the girls; I remember the particular terror of "spin the bottle" at parties, knowing I'd have to perform an ease and desire I didn't feel.

Despite all my best efforts, I sometimes got asked "Are you gay? Why do you walk like that, talk like that?" Every time I was asked the question, my stomach would knot, and I'd have to swallow my fear and anger.

Over time, these swallowed emotions became a heavy burden. I remember my dad asking me once, "Why do you have such a chip on your shoulder?" Even if I'd wanted to, there's no way I could have explained to him how broken I felt—how each expression of disapproval from my family and peers had chipped away a little bit at my soul.

I wish my dad and I could have found a way to talk to each other. His attempts to connect with me through sports always failed; I just didn't have the interest or ability. My dad had had a rough childhood, watching his mother get abused by a series of boyfriends. As an adult, he became a social worker, and he spent his days trying to help people navigate impossible situations: abuse, delinquency, addiction, homelessness. By the time he got home every day, he was exhausted, his patience already worn thin. Something as small as laughing too loudly at the dinner table could trigger him, and then he'd explode: his face would turn red, his neck veins bulging, and he'd bring his face close to mine and yell. Sometimes he'd hit me—though usually my sisters got spared (apparently my maleness made me a legitimate target for violence, or perhaps he held a deeper grudge against me for failing to meet his expectations for a son). My sisters and I constantly walked on eggshells, but we couldn't always anticipate, let alone prevent, his outbursts.

Once, I made the mistake of telling a teacher where I'd gotten a bruise, and my dad had to go in and speak to the counselor at school. At home, I got in trouble for having told. The lesson was clear: violence was always possible, but to talk about it—to recognize the fact out loud—was taboo. Much like other things and topics.

Now, looking back, I see that my dad was imprisoned by his own unmanageable feelings, which then became a cage for the rest of us. Vulnerability was not an option—expressing his feelings and asking for help would have broken the code of masculinity. But he'd never had a model for masculinity that didn't rely on violence.

Deep down, I knew that I didn't want any part of this.

But there were rules to the world I lived in, and it was within this world that I had to survive. I knew that there was no way for me to fully express myself without facing ridicule and violence—so I hid the parts of myself that I could, and developed armor to face the rest.

I started to live a double life, with the aid of the newly-existent Internet. I spent a lot of time talking to men in early AOL chat rooms, and sometimes I'd go meet them in person. I regularly snuck off in the middle of the night, completely unbeknownst to my parents. Sometimes I ran away to Boston or New York, or even Albany or Springfield—anything to find myself in a different place, where I could be anonymous and feel the tingle of possibility. One of the men I met online got me a fake ID, and I started going to clubs—though I still looked like I was twelve, the ID would earn me access to a tantalizing adult space, where, for a few precious hours, I could escape my life.

At school, I felt an increasing pressure to perform my straightness. Though I did my best, someone occasionally saw through the act. There was a code: if someone called you "gay," you had to fight them. Even if you lost the fight, that was better than "being a bitch," refusing to fight and ceding your claim to masculinity.

I continued to shapeshift in terms of my own personal style, trying to find ways to express myself within acceptable masculine parameters. I developed an alter ego I'll call "B.RAD," dressing in baggy pants like a rapper. I was obsessed with MTV; it was like my church. All I wanted was to be on MTV someday. I continued to long for a post-high-school time when I'd have the freedom to travel and explore, to discover more of who I was—to find a vocabulary for self-expression bigger than what I saw around me in Pittsfield. For now, music videos, with their proliferation of styles and larger-than-life personalities, provided that horizon.

Some of my friends started smoking pot, and I fell into a daily habit; eager to do anything to avoid the stigma of the potential "gay" label, I embraced the mantle of "pothead." One day, I was caught smoking with some classmates. Because I "snitched"—told the teachers which one of my peers had brought in the weed—they jumped me one night in the street. My friend Lauren watched, horrified, yelling for them to stop, but I came out of the experience completely traumatized, with bruises and a black eye.

After that, I decided to be more proactive about protecting myself, and I started to carry a knife around. One day I forgot that the knife was in my pocket, and sat on the couch. The knife pierced my body, tearing my urethra and severing an artery. I called for my mom; seeing the couch cushion soaked in blood, she was too shocked to call for help. "What's the number for 911?" she kept asking. "It's 911!" I screamed.

I ended up being airlifted to the hospital in Boston and having multiple surgeries and blood transfusions. I nearly died. I was in the hospital for a month. During my long recovery, I developed a fondness for Percocets and a fear of leaving the house. In some ways, this moment was a wake-up call: I knew I couldn't live the way I'd been living. The constant fear of violence had itself almost killed me.

I didn't know what the next step was, but luckily, a door out of my untenable situation opened when my family decided to move to Florida. The move would provide an escape hatch from the toxic social environment of Pittsfield and the bad influences surrounding me.

I barely finished high school before we moved; in fact, I almost didn't graduate because I had failed gym twice. I had to go to summer school to make up the credits.

In retrospect, it's obvious why I failed gym. It wasn't just that I didn't like sports: being a trans girl who had to change in the boys' locker room was traumatic. Every session of gym class was laden with triggers for fear and dysphoria. Now, seeing various schools get sued for failing to allow trans kids the use of bathrooms aligning with their gender identity, I still sometimes idly fantasize about suing the school district, some part of me longs for any recognition—however belated—that I always was a girl, a girl whose education failed her in more ways than one.

*My first fashion show at my grandma's. She would let us play in her closet and dress up. This was everything to me!*

*My fedora and brief case going to 3rd grade. I always wanted to play office and business.*

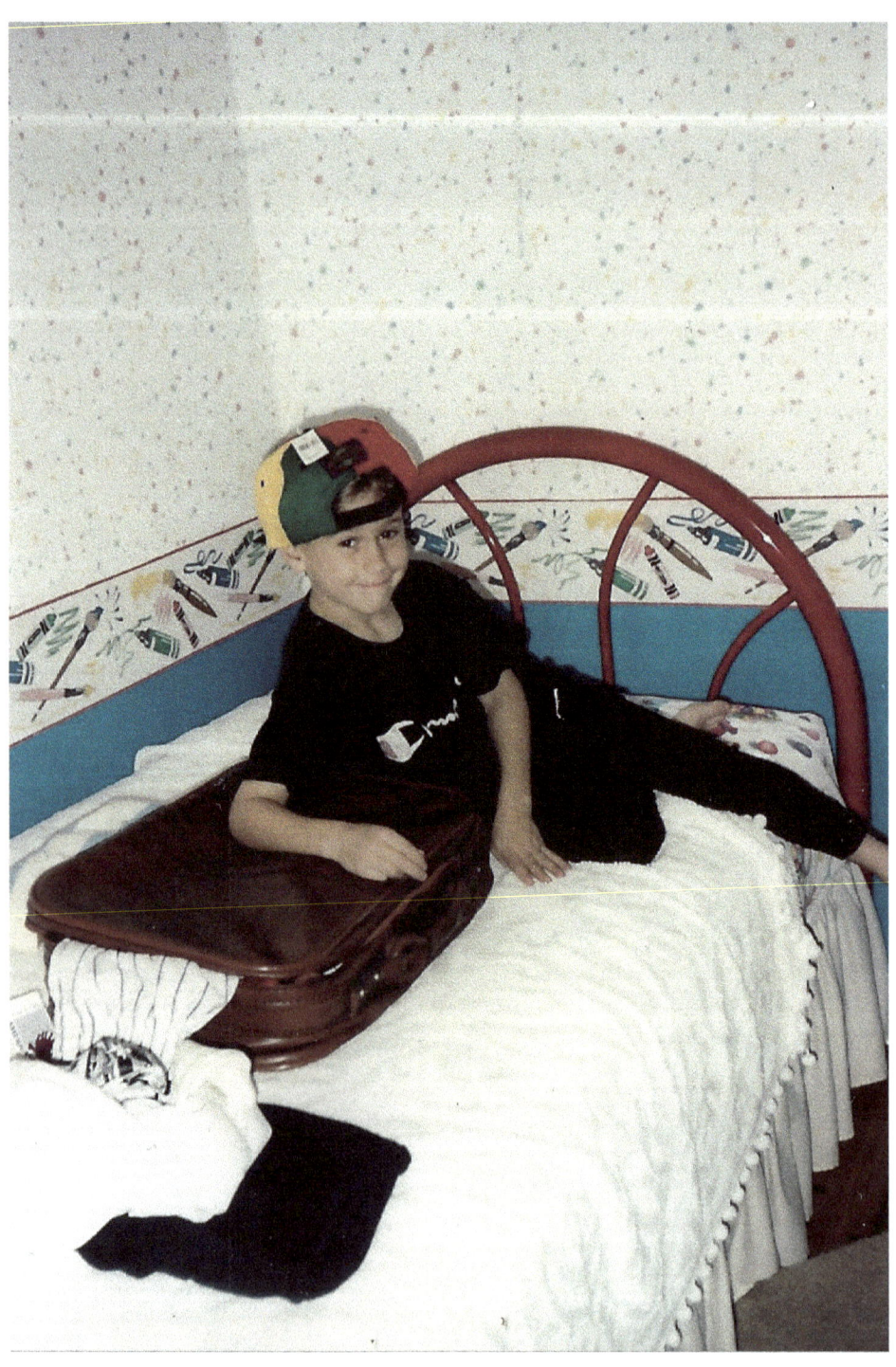

*My suitcase was always ready. I loved vacations and dreaming of far away lands. Packing for Disney World*

# 2

# BECOMING INDASHIO

## Designing The Dream

Throughout my childhood, I indulged my love of fashion mostly by proxy, through my younger sister Angel. Having learned early on that it wasn't acceptable to wear her clothes (or any clothes meant for girls), I settled for dressing and styling Angel on my own behalf. She became my muse. I'd choose her outfits for her, coming up with the most fabulous and surprising combinations of colors and textures. Thanks to her patience with my endless experiments, I learned to do hair, makeup, and nails; I'd spend time styling her in the morning and send her off to school dressed like Li'l Kim or Christina Aguilera. I'm endlessly grateful for her patience and her willingness to be my muse; she sometimes got teased at school for looking like she'd just stepped off the set of a booty-shaking music video, but she endured it with grace. I think she knew that I needed her.

## THIS LITTLE LIGHT OF MINE

In 2002, when my family moved to Florida, I started to perceive more potential outlets for my creative ambitions. I began experimenting with my own fashions: altering and repurposing thrift store clothes, piecing together surprising looks from found pieces. Once again, Angel was my most important muse. I was beginning to get a sense that fashion would be the way for me to build a name for myself while expressing who I was. I sought the larger stage I'd long dreamed of, and the chance to create the kind of dresses and outfits I'd always wanted to wear.

As I continued my experiments and began evolving a look, I came up with a name for my brand. Originally it was "Indigo," since I used a lot of denim: I'd find denim pieces at Goodwill and cut, bleach, deconstruct, repurpose them into something new. Somehow, "Indigo" evolved into the self-created name Indashio. I don't know where the name came from—I think it just found me. I loved the way it sounded: fresh, exotic, memorable, and unique. Over time, the brand's new moniker attached to my own name and personality. In a kind of "fake it to make it" gesture, I started introducing myself by saying, "Hi, I'm Indashio, and I'm a celebrity fashion designer"—long before the world recognized me as such. In retrospect, it wasn't so different from my childhood travel agency; though I had no training or credentials, my sheer confidence—my willingness to declare it already so—made things happen. I knew I was on a mission.

## THIS LITTLE LIGHT OF MINE

From the beginning, I hustled. I continually sent my designs to MTV, VH1, and BET; my dream was to see my clothes on the TV channels that obsessed me. I knew that my persistence would eventually pay off, and I was willing to endure rejection and indifference along the way.

I like to say now that "the things Brad couldn't do, Indashio could do." In some ways, Indashio was a character that I created and then inhabited—to give myself permission to grow past the confining expectations set for me in Pittsfield and express my personality on a wider stage. And it worked: in becoming Indashio and developing my skills as a designer, I finally had the outlet I'd been searching for. I got reactions from people that I'd never gotten before, and my self-esteem soared. I was spellbound by the force of my new persona, ready to take on the world.

Indashio was daring, courageous, and resourceful. Indashio never took "No" for an answer. Indashio was charismatic and skilled at building connections, a master networker. Indashio found ways to use whatever resources he found at his disposal; even if he had no money and the most meager of supplies, he found ways to repurpose, transform, and create something dazzling. Indashio was larger than life: like Madonna, he only needed one name. He never apologized for taking up space. Indashio knew he was good—and, more importantly, he knew that no one was more determined and hungry for success than he was. Indashio's confidence stunned and inspired others. Indashio was his own fiercest advocate, and he accomplished things that shouldn't have been possible. Indashio was a superhero.

All of this would come at a cost, of course. Though Indashio provided a crucial channel for some of my best qualities and allowed me to expand the borders of my previously cramped selfhood, he was still, at the end of the day, a persona—a character I was playing. Over time, the act would grow exhausting, and Indashio would struggle to stay alive. But that all came later.

## On The Catwalk

In 2003, I decided to have my first fashion show, in Miami. I made everything happen myself: endlessly cold-calling companies to solicit sponsorships, recruiting my sister and her friends as models.

I finally secured a sponsorship from Maybelline when I told the representative who answered my call, "Listen, you're the 200th person I've called—if you don't sponsor me, I'm gonna kill myself." "Oh my goodness, don't do that!" she responded. In the end, they didn't give me money, but they sent me free makeup, and we established a rapport and relationship that would continue after the show. I also connected with a representative from Candies. I loved their shoes, and I appreciated the work that their foundation was doing to reduce teen pregnancy. The slogan was, "Just because you're sexy doesn't mean you have to have sex." It made me think of so many of my friends from Pittsfield who had already become mothers. I liked the idea of using my show to promote a charity and made a commitment to do so with every show in the future.

At the time, I was still living with my parents; when large boxes would arrive at our door—shipments of makeup from Maybelline, shoes from Candies—they had a lot of questions: "What exactly are you doing? It's not illegal, is it?"

The show took place during Fashion Week, in a tent across from the Versace Mansion. I couldn't believe I'd made it here: Miami buzzed with audacious energy, and I was surrounded by the people and brands I'd only seen before on TV or in magazines.

The day of the show, I felt as alive as I've ever felt. I was the ringleader of the whole operation, bringing my designs to life on a stage where they could be celebrated. I came up with not only the clothes, but the entire vision; I found the models, oversaw their hair and makeup. Seeing my creations on a real runway was thrilling beyond anything I'd ever experienced. I knew I had found my calling.

My whole family had come to see the show; afterwards, they wanted to celebrate back at the hotel, but I dismissed them, telling them I'd invited the models from the show to an afterparty in my room. My family drove back home to Tampa, and in the end, no one came to my afterparty. I ended up sitting alone in my beautiful hotel room suite, wishing that my family was still there. In some ways, this moment now seems like a foreshadowing of Indashio's narrative arc; he always put his career and networking first, and sometimes pushed away the people who loved him in the process. But that day, even the loneliness of my hotel room suite couldn't dampen the fulfilled, victorious feeling I had: I knew, now, that I could bring my visions to life. I was on my way.

For a budding, ravenously ambitious fashion designer, New York City was the obvious next step. I learned online about a small designer market happening in the Meatpacking District, and I paid the fee—$200 or so—to enter. I packed a trunk full of my clothes and headed to the Big Apple.

What I remember most clearly about that day was that, to my own delight, someone bought one of my shirts! This was what I'd come for, of course, but I still couldn't believe that someone in New York had paid 80 dollars for one of my creations—actually one of my sister's old T-shirts, onto which I'd sewn a dollar-store flower. Because I had no money and very few resources, all of my clothes were like this: recycled garments from Goodwill or my sister's closet, remixed and re-stitched by my own self-taught hands. So when someone actually paid money for one of my pieces, I felt like I'd won the lottery.

I loved New York; it felt like an island full of talented misfits, all as hungry and ambitious as myself. I came back several times to do trunk shows (my ticket sometimes funded by another Internet boyfriend, who lived in Connecticut), and I started to build connections.

On one of these trips, I went to the offices of Vibe magazine for a long-sought meeting. I'd been calling their offices for months, asking to meet their fashion director. Finally he said, "OK, what do I have to do to get you to stop calling me?" I responded: "I'd like a 30-minute meeting, I want to show you my clothes, and I'd like you to put them in the magazine." He said, "I'll give you a 10-minute meeting; I'll look at your clothes, but no promises." I said I'd take it. At the meeting, he went through my trunk of clothes, briskly evaluating each piece: "This is shit, this is shit, this is shit... this one is OK, this one is actually kind of amazing." For someone like me, who'd never gone to fashion school, feedback even as hurried and brusque as this was invaluable; I took his advice to heart. I continued to harass him, and though he never did put me in the magazine, I remained on his radar; he knew who I was.

In these early New York days, I met Rob, who had a showroom on Fashion Avenue and would become my manager. He offered to represent me, and told me that he'd like for me to do a show at New York fashion week—but it would cost $2,500 to register. Around this time, I also reconnected with a friend from Pittsfield, who was dating a fast-talking Casanova type who happened to manage the rap group Onyx. Early in our acquaintance, he took note of my ambition and potential and decided to help me out (as I was beginning to learn, Indashio's confidence was contagious). When he met pretty girls, as he often did in his line of work, he'd ask them, "Do you want to model for my friend, the up-and-coming designer Indashio?" When I told him about my ambition to do a show at New York fashion week, he offered to pay the registration fee.

Thanks to him, I found myself the youngest participant in the designer showcase at New York Fashion Week that year. I was only nineteen. I knew that this could be a big break for me, but I had no money and very few resources; I'd have to do what I could to generate buzz on my own. At the time, I was working the night shift at a hotel in Clearwater, Florida, and I used my shifts to prepare for the show: sewing clothes, printing and faxing press kits. When the manager berated us—"Where is all this printer ink going?"—I just kept my mouth shut.

If I'd ever doubted the cutthroat nature of the fashion world, that first Fashion Week show made it clear. I learned that if you want to be the best, your scissors have to stay sharp. Having so many up-and-coming designers in a room, all with egos as large (or almost) as mine, was like crabs in a bucket: all of us climbing all over each other, seeking every scrap of attention and access. I remember fighting with another designer about which of us would be able to use Beyoncé music, and of course I won.

We worked with established hair and makeup artists, but

all of the models were shared, so we had to find ways to make our designs stand out using models with similar looks. I developed a rivalry with one other designer in particular, Estaban Cortazar. It was like we knew that there would only be room for one of us. He was good, but I knew that I wanted it more. I was going to be the one. When I saw someone else getting attention, I became a master at redirecting it toward myself and my designs: "Y'all are looking in the wrong place. This, over here, is it."

I wasn't delusional; I knew I wasn't the best designer in the room. For starters, I lacked the training most of them had; I hadn't been to fashion school, had taught myself how to sew. However, I was the best at self-promotion and business. These other designers were really creative, but they wouldn't get on the phone to call anybody. Though I had a manager, I was also my own manager. If there was an editor or celebrity in the room, I was going to go up and introduce myself and make sure they knew who I was. I spent countless hours on the phone, cold-calling fashion editors, publicists, producers, and marketing VPs, and asking for what I wanted. Not every ask worked out, but I knew that it was this audacity, diligence, and networking ability that would eventually set me apart.

I had my first interview soon after that, with Lucire, an up-and-coming fashion magazine from New Zealand. Jack, the publisher, became an important person in my life—one of those dots that connect and form the constellation of people who can support a growing dream.

Another important person I ended up meeting during this time—at my Fashion Week afterparty in the Meatpacking district, at a club called Lotus—was a friend I'll call Riri. I first noticed her because of her look: she was wearing an amazing outfit, admittedly designed by one of the other designers, but with a layer of personal style that took it to the next level. She was dating a well-known rapper and had a TV show on the local network MNN (Manhattan Neighborhood Network), which was pretty big at the time. From the moment I met her that night we were fast friends. Initially she may have wanted something more—she came up to my hotel room, and I had to tell her "I don't play for that team"—but we soon became an unstoppable duo. Riri was just like me: bold, fearless, and unapologetic. Everywhere we went, people recognized her. She was an amazing muse. She'd wear anything, with total confidence and panache. People couldn't take their eyes off her. We went out every night, crashing any industry party we learned about. At clubs, she'd always end up in the middle of the dance floor, executing Cirque du Soleil-level moves. In this way, alongside Riri, I met even more people and drew them into my orbit.

Riri was living with a girl named Jen in Washington Heights, and she invited me to move in. Though the house was pretty disgusting—roaches, piss smell, the works—it was a free place to stay. Finally we got a different place, moving in with a Dominican family in Harlem. I loved living in Harlem, though when I walked around, sometimes I'd get called "Boy George": "Hey, Boy George, go take your ass to the Village."

Riri would sometimes steal my clothes, but I loved it; she was the first person who'd really, truly loved them. She didn't care that I hadn't gone to fashion school, that everything was a bit DIY and rough around the edges. She'd wear them out in the world, with her signature style, and people would notice. When someone asked, "What are you wearing?" she'd tell them all about Indashio.

At the next year's Fashion Week, I was able to get a press pass through Lucire; Riri and I showed up at every party and worked the room. Around this time, I started to get some resistance from the IMG producers (IMG was the company that produced Fashion Week). They didn't like that I was an outsider, trying to fight my way to the center of the fashion world. It's true that I was loud and audacious, but to them it must have looked like I was taking up far more space than I had any right to—a young hooligan running amok. I was almost kicked out several times. I'd always show them my press pass, point to my name on the list, and they'd reluctantly allow me to stay. But I could tell that they did not want me there. I was nineteen, twenty, and often the youngest person there.

I did meet one woman named Toni who became an amazing, fabulous friend and mentor. She had a nonprofit organization called Entertainers for Education. She gave me my first sponsorship money, and asked me to customize some clothes for her. She gave me some seed money and a sponsorship deck. I started soliciting sponsors, and every season I got more.

Over the next year or so, my persistence began to pay off. I finally got some of my clothes worn by VJs on MTV and VH1, and this started to build some buzz. My clothes were spotted on celebrities. I was profiled in 2004 by Women's Wear Daily.

All of this was thrilling, of course. Indashio's signature confidence was like a magic spell: as long as I believed in my powers of manifestation, I could make almost anything happen. As I accumulated an orbit of followers, as my work gained recognition, I could feel myself approaching the goal I'd set: to become utterly self-sufficient, so famous and rich that everyone wouldn't be able to help but love me.

I was only partly aware of it at the time, but this was the core motivation for my turbo-charged ambition: to be accepted, to be loved. I thought that if I were only rich and famous enough, it wouldn't matter who I was—not my body, not my gender identity, not the ways in which I'd failed to meet the expectations set for me early in life. If I couldn't earn acceptance and love simply by being myself, then perhaps I could earn it through hard work, success, and the sheer glittering force of Indashio's charisma.

THIS LITTLE LIGHT OF MINE

## Making Money, Making Magic

Of course, while I was chasing my dreams and networking with New York's finest and most fabulous, I was still essentially broke, living in a fifth floor walkup. I needed some way to pay the bills.

My first New York job was as a telemarketer for a company that sold duct tape to shipping companies. I lasted maybe a week there: it became immediately clear to me that the company was sketchy, and that I was essentially being asked to con people into a scam.

Soon after that, I learned about a job opening at the AIDS Walk organization. It involved going door to door to raise awareness for the walk, putting up posters, and knocking on doors. The money was good—$25 per hour—and each shift included a free meal.

Still, I resisted the work. I had grown up terrified of AIDS, especially since I'd been encouraged by my family and the surrounding culture to associate the disease with homosexuality. I still had a huge amount of internalized homophobia; I avoided mannerisms that coded as queer, refrained from using words like "fierce." Some part of me still saw queerness as a contagion, a pathology to be avoided at all costs.

Now, pushing a cart of posters through the city and knocking on doors for AIDS Walk, I was aware that most people I interacted with would assume not only that I was gay but that I had AIDS myself. In anticipating and encountering their reactions, I felt the full force and weight of the stigma, and became uncomfortably aware of the self-loathing that stigma had bred in me.

I remember one particular day when I felt thoroughly discouraged. I was pushing the cart of AIDS Walk literature through the West Village—hungry and exhausted from dragging the unwieldy metal contraption through various neighborhoods, onto and off of subways and buses, all the while feeling its metaphorical as well as its literal weight. Surviving in New York—just paying the rent, let alone having the energy to dream and compete—was sometimes just as difficult as everyone said it would be.

I passed a restaurant with outdoor tables; some cash was sitting on one of the sidewalk tables, not yet picked up by the waiter. Without thinking, I reached out and pocketed it. After turning the corner, shame blossomed through me when I realized what I'd done out of sheer unthinking desperation. I vowed to pay the money back someday.

Just then, I passed the storefront window of Patricia Fields—a costume designer and wardrobe stylist I greatly admired at the time, known for outfitting "Sex and the City." To my own shock and elation, one of my own tops was displayed in the window! They were the first store in New York to place an order for my clothes.

This moment felt like an epiphany. Just when I'd been so discouraged that I'd nearly been ready to give up, seeing that shirt in the window was like a sign that I was on the right track after all. In that moment, I vowed not to give up until I'd achieved the fame I dreamed of. Even if I had to be hungry, or homeless, or exhaust myself trying, it would be worth it, to prove myself in New York's creative crucible.

My second season at New York Fashion Week, it was a grassroots, low-budget affair, but my manager Rob mentored me thoughtfully, pairing me with an excellent illustrator and helping me create sellable pieces that were properly sketched and capably made. I called it my "Candy Collection." MTV covered it, and I was approached by the producers of a TV pilot called "Teens in Fashion."

After that, I went to LA for the first time; I did a Fashion Week show at the Mondrian Hotel in West Hollywood. I felt like I was finally getting the attention I wanted. Everything was sponsored; and celebrities were in and at my show; I had orders from several LA clothing stores.

That LA show was my first time working with the Make-a-Wish foundation. Since working with the Candies foundation at my very first show, I'd always seen my shows as opportunities to give back. This time I contacted Make-a-Wish, and they connected me with a girl named Sheena, who had sickle cell anemia and whose dream was to be a model. They flew her to LA, and I put her in my show. It made me feel so good to grant this wish that I did it again, at several of my subsequent shows.

After LA, I went back to Miami; I'd heard about a new

show that was filming, called "8th & Ocean," and I wanted to get on. I called the producers and the agency, and got some of their models in my next show. Though the show in fact never aired, it was another opportunity for me to make some great connections.

Around this time, I started to feel like a sorcerer. Though I was barely making enough money to cover my expenses, people were willing to do almost anything for me for free; Indashio had a persuasive way of convincing people that just the experience of working with him, being a part of his orbit, would be worth it. As my reputation built—a sense that this kid Indashio was really doing things—my sense of my own power and personal pull only grew.

And I myself was endlessly resourceful, unwilling to take no for an answer. One perfect example of this was my "Rags to Riches" show, in 2006. Two weeks out from the show, I still lacked a venue, and had no money to rent one. Seemingly out of nowhere, like a voice whispered in my ear, I got the idea to call Commerce Bank and ask them to sponsor me. The VP told me "We won't sponsor you, but if you do the show in our bank, we'll pay for everything." I couldn't believe it—the location was unorthodox, but it fit the show's theme perfectly. The show was a smashing success; MTV covered it, and the bank offered in advance to sponsor me the next year.

Always hunting for ways to build my profile despite my lack of capital, I offered to do pro bono shoots for Lucire if they'd put my images on the cover. I called in favors, bartered, made connections, and managed to pull off $10,000 shoots for next to nothing. My triumph was arranging a shoot with Nicky Hilton, sister of Paris, who was the biggest celebrity at the time. Nicky agreed to do the shoot if she could wear her own clothes—she had a new fashion line she was promoting. I was able to shoot singer Vanessa Carlton as well (she was initially reluctant to wear my clothes, but eventually came around).

After the Nicky Hilton cover came out, and my "Rags to Riches" show aired on MTV's Made, my profile raised dramatically. I was soon approached and offered a chance to shoot an emerging star named Kim Kardashian. (At the time, she was mostly famous for a sex tape, but there were rumors that she'd be the new It Girl). Of course I said yes—though, again, I had a miniscule budget. I called in more favors, employing friends to do hair and makeup. Initially despondent at the thought of how to dress Kim—I lacked the funds to create the kind of bespoke outfit a celebrity like her would typically expect—I had an epiphany the night before the shoot. I was staying with my sister in Tampa at the time, and I noticed some sheer curtains hanging from her window. In a moment worthy of Gone with the Wind, I pulled the curtains down and started sewing. That's how I ended up dressing Kim Kardashian in a gown made of curtains. Kim was a dream to work with; she was totally game for the Louise Brooks-style bob I put her in, and if she noticed that I was dressing her in repurposed window-dressings, she never said so.

My next highlight was a show at one of my dream venues: the Versace mansion in Miami (the opportunity came about when I called in yet another favor: Christian, a DJ I'd befriended, worked there). It seemed like an incredible full-circle moment; my very first show had taken place in a tent across the street, and now my designs would be shown in the mansion itself. This was my "To Die For" collection (which I privately dubbed the "Edward Scissorhands" collection, because everything was artfully shredded). Once again, I featured models from the Make-a-Wish foundation; my publicist was able to snag them $500 gift cards, so I took them on a dream shopping spree before the event.

Thrilled that I'd scored such a fabulous venue, I knew that I needed to drum up as much press as possible. I was dreaming big—as in not just the Miami Herald, but national press. Without much of a budget, I needed a stunt.

The opportunity to get the word out came only after the show itself had already happened. I got a call asking if I had a dress that might fit Kelly Rowland, of Destiny's Child, for a shoot she was doing. "I have just the thing," I said, thinking of a dress that had appeared in the "To Die For" show. But after ransacking all of my suitcases, I couldn't find the dress I had in mind. This was when I had my lightbulb moment. I filed a police report and sent out a press release: $10,000 reward to anyone who finds Kelly Rowland's missing dress!

The story made it onto news channels from Miami to New York. "The case of the missing dress" became a sensation because Kelly Rowland's name was attached to it—but of course it got my name out there as well (mentioned in the same breath as the Versace Mansion, no less). Though the whole thing was essentially a joke (and I did find the dress in one of my suitcases, weeks later) it succeeded in putting my name on people's lips.

## Deals With The Devil

Despite my success and increasing popularity, I was starting to make some enemies. I had finally been kicked out of fashion week, after some genuinely bad behavior—incensed at being asked to give up my seat in the front row, I'd thrown a drink in someone's face. I was banned from future Fashion Week events; even Kim Kardashian didn't have enough sway to get me in (she tried to take me to an event after our shoot, but I was spotted and asked to leave).

Another incident that earned me some notoriety was my attempt to get on the design competition reality show "Project Runway." They'd announced an open call for auditions, but when I showed up and saw the line stretching around the block, I thought there was no way in hell I'd stand on that line all day just for the chance to be seen. Certain that I'd earned the cachet to cut the line, I did just that. When they asked me to wait at the back of the line, I demanded to speak to whoever was in charge, and refused to leave until security kicked me out. I ended up causing such a scene that my antics earned a mention in Women's Wear Daily. (Needless to say, I wasn't chosen for the show).

The truth was that Indashio's ego was getting out of control. Finally having achieved some of the notoriety he'd dreamed of, he only became hungry for more—and he was willing to do almost anything to climb higher.

I started to get a reputation for being high maintenance and full of myself. The tide of my popularity hadn't turned yet, but some people were beginning to be wary of me.

My next big break—the biggest break of Indashio's career—would come about in part because of this bad reputation. I was flown to LA to audition for a reality show called "Glam Gods" on VH1; when I brought Indashio's signature drama to my audition, swirling in and out of the studio like the Tasmanian Devil, the producers must have rubbed their hands together in glee. I was perfect reality TV material.

The show was hosted by Vivica A. Fox. Its premise was inspired by US Weekly's "best-dressed/worst-dressed" feature; twelve contestants, all designers and stylists, competed to get our clients onto the "best dressed" list. I lived with the other contestants for the weeks of filming—somehow living out my childhood fantasy of being on "The Real World," but with all of my real-life problems.

The experience of actually being on a reality TV show

is a bit like being a rat in a maze: motivated by the highly visible cheese, never able to rest, constantly watched and evaluated by those on the outside. I began to go stir-crazy in the house—and, in my determination to win, I lost my grip on what remained of my moral compass.

The "reality" of reality TV is, of course, not very real at all; the producers are constantly manipulating contestants behind the scenes. Toward the end of the competition, the producers—who wanted to keep me on the show—told me what to do to win a particular challenge. It was a challenge where we had to work in pairs; the producers snuck me tips of what the judges did and didn't want to see, and I essentially threw my partner under the bus. Everything they disliked about the look was attributed to him, and he was sent home.

I did feel badly about sabotaging that designer; my heart broke a little bit when he left. I knew that he wanted to win just as badly as I did. I consoled myself by telling myself that we couldn't all be the Glam God—and that no one, after all, was more qualified or more destined for success than me. Hadn't I earned this?

In the end, I won the competition. Of course, there was a delay between the moment when I knew I'd won the show and the moment when it aired (and I wouldn't get paid until then). So for months, I had the strange experience of knowing that I'd just achieved the biggest success of my career but being unable to cash in on it, literally or figuratively. I was strictly forbidden from telling anyone the outcome of the show (I broke the rule only once, telling my roommate V—I had to tell someone—but otherwise was able to keep my mouth shut).

During this period, back in New York, I did yet another fashion show in which my resourcefulness made up for my lack of funds. I called this one my "Paper Doll Collection"; the clothes and wigs were all made out of newspaper. The show got a lot of attention. Two years later, when Cher did a music video with wigs made out of paper, I liked to imagine I'd inspired her.

The prize for winning Glam God was $100,000. When the check finally came, it brought relief but also anxiety and pressure. I'd never seen money like that before in my life. Everybody wanted money, from family to friends. My friend V ended up suing me because she believed she deserved a portion of the winnings, having served as my sometimes muse and collaborator. Unfortunately, that ruined our friendship.

I knew one thing for sure: I was no longer going to make do living in a squalid walk-up. I pre-paid a year's worth of rent on a penthouse on Fifth Avenue in East Harlem, and invited my sister to live there with me. It had two bedrooms, two bathrooms, and a gold hot tub—engraved with my name, no less—in the living room.

Best of all, after the show aired, I started to be recognized by strangers on the street—and not only in LA and New

York! I remember once being spotted in an airport in South Africa and marveling that my image had been broadcast, and was now recognizable, all over the world.

In other words, by anyone's definition, I had finally "made it." But of course, like a fairy-tale heroine who achieves success through a deal with the devil, mine would come at a cost. I'd spent so many years feeding Indashio's ego—stoking the outsized persona I needed to create success out of essentially thin air—that it had now grown, like wildfire, past all reasonable proportions. My ego had become unsatisfiable, almost monstrous. Now that I had money and recognition, it was too late to rein it in.

THIS LITTLE LIGHT OF MINE

*INDA:SHIO top in Patricia Field SoHo Store 2005. It was an unexpected dream come true.*

*2005 Miami Funkshion Fashion Week "Rags to Riches Collection."
I sewed this collection by hand on the floor of my walkup.*

*New York Fashion Week (FW05). Camilia Alves, February 2005, wearing Rags to Riches Collection.*

*In a "Gone with the Wind" moment I made this dress out of curtains the night before. Kim is the perfect muse. Miami 2007*

*Kim was such a great muse she could wear anything and make it look good.*

THIS LITTLE LIGHT OF MINE

*New York Fashion Week Viva Las Vegas collection September 2007*

THIS LITTLE LIGHT OF MINE

*Winning Glam God changed my life. Pictured on the finale with Vivica Fox holding the check in 2008*

*NYFW 2010 AMBER & INDASHIO wearing my first pair of heels on the catwalk for my Club Kid Collection.*

# 3

## END OF AN ERA

## The Brink

My Glam God winnings were gone in a month and a half. Not to be deterred, I started booking appearance fees in cities across the country, sometimes even internationally. I was finally making money through sponsorships and endorsements.

Still, there were parts of myself I carefully hid from the world. I'd begun cross-dressing when I was alone at home, when my sister was out. I started shaving my legs, painting my toenails. I'd started to think of this version of myself as a new persona I called "Courtney." I had a pink dress that I loved, and I thought about wearing it to my next show, in the Bahamas. I remember sitting in the vanity of my hotel room, trying to get up the courage. But as bold and fearless as Indashio could be, as much as he loved pushing the envelope and attracting attention for his audacity, wearing a dress in public felt like one step too far. While inhabiting the persona of Indashio, I'd pulled far more audacious stunts than wearing a dress—but this wasn't just a stunt. It was who I was. Ultimately, it felt too vulnerable. I think I was afraid that if I allowed myself to fully embrace my femininity, Indashio himself would crumble.

In the end, I settled for a compromise. The collection I was showing was called "Party Monster," based on the film with Macaulay Culkin. The collection's aesthetic was based on that of the club kids in the movie—glitter, bold makeup, and plenty of androgyny. Under the mantle of the collection, I could push the envelope a bit without going so far as wearing a dress. I ended up shaping my hair into a blue Mohawk and sporting Kiss-style platform heels. People loved it; I felt like a rock star.

That success earned me my first big sponsorship, from Trident; finally I was able to execute my vision with the funding I needed. Even better, the show itself was the type I'd gotten kicked out of when I was just starting out: the big tent, the A-list celebrities, covered by the Wall Street Journal and Page 6. I called this my Liberace collection; it was all about "God and Gaudiness." The models strutted down the catwalk to Madonna's "Like a Prayer" and Belinda Carlisle's "Heaven is a Place on Earth," and Lady Gaga's "Born this way," all songs I played while sewing and creating it.

Clearly, my ego wasn't showing any signs of shrinking. If anything, it was growing more monstrous: cannibalizing whatever it needed in order to keep Indashio's persona alive, to help his profile grow ever larger.

I started openly being a diva—sometimes just for the sake of being a diva. I think on some level, I saw it as a kind of self-fulfilling prophecy: the more important I acted, the more important I would become. I yelled at DJs when I thought they'd gotten the music wrong; I berated backstage staff; I started ignoring the people around me who weren't at least as famous and well-connected as I was, who couldn't help me get ahead. If you weren't a celebrity or industry insider, I stopped being able to see you.

The truth was that the fame and success wasn't what I thought it would be. The more popular I got, and the more notoriety I got, the emptier I felt. As thrilling as it was to see my name and designs out in the world, it didn't get me what I really wanted: acceptance and love, from others and—most importantly—from myself. But even if I had been able to fully admit this to myself, I wouldn't have known how to stop. Intuitively I knew that if I stopped to self-reflect, I'd self-destruct; as Indashio, I only knew how to seek more, go bigger.

In my private life, the cracks in Indashio's persona were becoming more obvious. I was cross-dressing more and more often at home. On some level I was aware that Courtney and Indashio were incompatible, so I kept Courtney to myself.

During this time I also fell in love. It had been a long time since I'd been in a relationship, and I fell hard for a guy. Though the relationship didn't last long, it showed me how deeply I yearned to love and be loved. I called my next collection "The Love Collection" in an attempt to express this theme and try to manifest some change in my personal life—but in retrospect I see how clearly I was failing to love myself, to love those around me. Expressing my heart through a fashion show wasn't going to cut it anymore, as much as I might pretend.

## Burning It Down

As these cracks in Indashio's façade became apparent, my professional fortunes started to turn. My next business venture did not go as well as I'd hoped. I started a line for men called "Male Polish," with nail polishes marketed to men, its signature color "Indashio Black"; despite some positive press, the collection didn't sell.

I soon found that I'd run out of money. Unable to pay my rent, I got evicted from my penthouse. I couldn't even take my personalized hot tub with me—the movers couldn't figure out how to get it out. The metaphorical undertones were all too obvious. Once again I found myself living in a Washington Heights walkup (though I still had the money to pay for a separate office).

During this time, I auditioned and was cast on another reality show—this one called "24 Hour Catwalk," on Lifetime. This time, my bad attitude didn't end up working out for me; I was so obviously the show's villain that the producers felt the need to bust my ego on national TV. I ended up losing the show. I didn't go down quietly—I left in a stream of profanity, threatening to sue the show's producers, who promised me a spinoff but never followed through.

Somehow, over all this time, I had never come out to my parents—and though my sexuality was probably obvious already, on "24 Hour Catwalk," it was undeniable. I finally sat my mother down after 27 years of shame and hiding to have the conversation.

When I said "Mom, there's something I have to tell you," she looked petrified. "I want you to know," I continued, "That I'm gay. I always have been, I've wanted to tell you but haven't known how. I just want you to love and accept me."

She immediately looked relieved; I'm not sure what she'd thought I was about to say. "We've always known you were gay," she said reassuringly. "We don't care, we just want you to be happy."

This wasn't the worst this conversation could have gone, of course, but I felt incredibly angry: they'd known all this time, and pretended not to? Over the years I'd been asked countless times, at countless family gatherings, whether or not I had a girlfriend. Why had they kept up this charade, watching me twist and distort myself in an attempt to earn their love and acceptance? Still, it was a relief to be out, and I was grateful that the show—however disastrously it had turned out—had forced me to finally have the conversation.

As if to underscore the incompatibility of Courtney and Indashio, my manager had secured an investor and manufacturing partner and urged me to create a men's collection as my next professional move. Since my profile had grown to the point where my clothes would actually be sold in stores like Nordstrom, I had to both "tone it down" and "man up." There was pressure to create homogeneous clothes that reinforced traditional masculine aesthetics, rather than pushing the envelope.

Having been told my whole life that I needed to "man up" in order to fit in, it felt like my spirit was being killed all over again. My audacity might have earned me success, but now, in order to maintain that success, I was once again having to hide. My spirit balked at the prospect, and I grew depressed. At the afterparty, I should have felt happy; celebrities were there, everyone was congratulating me, the collection had been a success. But I just felt dead inside.

Soon after that, a conflict between my sister (who'd long been working on my team) and my manager forced me to choose between my professional representation and my family. My sister had just found out she was pregnant, by my manager's ex-boyfriend. Though my relationship with my sister was strained by that point, as well—and matters weren't helped when I advised her to get an abortion, worried about her pregnancy's consequences for my career—in the end I chose her. This resulted in a bridge with my manager burnt, a cascade of canceled contracts, and a lot of money down the drain. At that point, though, I felt utterly numb, willing to sabotage myself. It was hard to see the value in the hustle anymore.

I did pull off one final audacious stunt, mustering every last remaining bit of Indashio's daring. My friend Eva and I decided to do a guerrilla fashion show at Grand Central Terminal for our "Wish Upon a Star" collection. I got the Hyatt Hotel next door to sponsor me, cashing in on Indashio's reputation, despite the fact that I hadn't secured any of the necessary permits (a fact I conveniently failed to mention when securing the sponsorship).

The day of the show, I got a call from the New York Police Commissioner. They'd somehow learned about my plans, and their message was clear: "Don't even think about doing it."

Indashio, of course, was not to be deterred. I gave my team a pep talk: "Listen, just do as I say: we're gonna just walk in, walk out. Don't linger." Somehow, we made it happen. I remember jumping up and down on the sidewalk with everyone afterwards: "We did it!"

Though not technically my last show, I now think of this illegal performance as Indashio's swan song. Though it carried some desperate overtones—as though I had to prove to myself I could still pull off something like that, despite my heart not being fully in it—it was one last chance for Indashio to embody the most audacious, unapologetic version of himself.

By that point, I was, in effect, homeless—unable to pay rent, I was squatting in my old office. Despite my decade working in fashion, despite some stunning successes, I was as broke and broken as I'd ever been. How was I back in this situation, barely able to afford food? Far from the idealistic nineteen-year-old who'd arrived starry-eyed in Manhattan a decade before, willing to starve in order to chase my dreams, I was now over 30 and exhausted.

In a final bid at resuscitating my TV career, I conceived of a show called "Catwalk Across America." I got a $10,000 sponsor to shoot a shoestring pilot in Alaska, marshaling all of my connections to get it made—but in the end it was a flop, and didn't get picked up. I was devastated, of course, but the outcome also somehow felt inevitable.

I had come to accept by that point, if only privately, that I needed to transition. As helpful as it had been to think of "Courtney" as just a character, I knew deep down that I'd been a woman all along, and I was finally starting to admit it to myself.

In other words, Indashio was dying. The engine wouldn't start, my magic tricks no longer worked. I simultaneously resisted it and allowed it to happen. It was terrifying to imagine who I'd be if I couldn't be Indashio anymore—I certainly couldn't go back to being Brad. But on some level I must have known that the persona I'd so effortfully built would need to crumble into ash before a truer self could arise, like a phoenix, in its place.

## Purgatory

I found myself, in 2014, back in my parents' house in Pittsfield. I'd given up my office, and essentially turned my back on what remained of my career.

The house was full—and full of tension. My sister, who'd also moved home, had given birth to my nephew. Though the baby turned out to be a gift and a joy, my relationship with my sister was strained. I'd mistreated her for far too long, abusing her affection and taking her for granted. The tension between us drove my mother crazy.

That Christmas, I didn't even have the money to buy my family gifts. I didn't feel worthy of receiving anything, either. I was miserable. I decided to write down "gifts of the future": what I planned to buy for each of my family members when I was successful and rich again. Louboutins for one sister, a car for the other, a Hawaii vacation for my parents. My family's reactions to these "gifts" were mixed; some appreciated the thought, while others laughed or looked puzzled.

As for me, I'd never felt this low before. It was obvious to everyone. I remember my aunt taking me for a walk and asking, "What's going on with you? It's really hard to see you like this—something's gotta change." I couldn't help but feel resentful at this late-breaking concern; my current depression was only the latest manifestation of a struggle I'd been fighting since I was born. They'd always thought I was crazy for pursuing such an unconventional life, without fully understanding the reasons behind any of it. Now I found myself exhausted, just as misunderstood as always.

During this time, I thought often of suicide. Without any money, it was hard to feel I had value, and I couldn't see a way back to meaningful participation in the world. I'd given my whole life to fashion, and completely lacked other skills. Often, it was only the thought of my baby nephew that kept me back from the brink.

Luckily, I soon met two people I think of as angels. One was my friend Eva, a designer who came from a wealthy background; she invited me to stay with her until I got back on my feet. It was on Eva's couch, watching the show "Transparent," that I first had the opportunity to come out to a trusted friend. "Do you think you might be trans?" she asked gently as the credits rolled.

It seems worth emphasizing that Eva would never have known to ask me that question if not for the show. Seeing a trans woman's life empathetically depicted onscreen— including her childhood struggle to fit in with the other kids who saw her as a boy—was so educational: not only did it teach cis people about trans people's experiences, but it allowed closeted trans people like me to see our experience reflected onscreen and find the courage to name who we were.

"Yes," I told Eva. "I think I am."

She went into the other room, came out with a dress, and handed it to me. "Here you go," she said. "Let's go out tonight."

My other "angel" was Kinyarda, a publicist turned entrepreneur who also housed me when I had few other options. She allowed me to stay at her house for three full years while I began my transition.

It was both terrifying and thrilling for me to go out on the town with her, wearing Indashio dresses—finally able to be my own muse and start dressing myself. After a while, though, I started to notice that it wasn't always easy for Kinyarda to be out with me. Seeing her with me, sometimes people assumed she was trans too and misgendered her or gave her strange looks. As a Black woman, she was used to being marginalized, and now she had to contend with another stigma, even just by association. I was grateful for the way she stuck with me throughout the process, even when it was challenging for her. I don't know who I'd be without her and Eva; their friendship and generosity allowed me the space and grace I needed to begin to transition.

*The Glam God at AXDW in Athens 2011.*
*The producers asked me not to wear this but I did anyway for press.*

*Athens Designer Exclusive Fashion Week 2011. One of my biggest victories.*

THIS LITTLE LIGHT OF MINE

*Nassau, Bahamas 2010 Club Kid Collection. This was a very courageous day putting on the pink dress.*

*INDASHIO Decade MTV Collection 2013 NYFW. Celebrating 10 years of fashion*

*New York Fashion Week SS13 Sept. 2012 American Dream Collection.*

*Alaska Fashion Week 2014 in Anchorage. Models wearing the Warrior Collection filming Catwalk Across America pilot.*

*My Nan would always come to Fashion Week and my shows. Her glamour always inspired me.*

THIS LITTLE LIGHT OF MINE

*This superhero also wore a cape!*
*2011 Trident Show at NYFW inspired by GOD, LIBERACE and GAUDINESS.*
*A thank you prayer.*

*NYFW 2013 Wish Upon a Start Collection at Grand Central Terminal: The Black Swan moment*

*Hosting Design Genius was amazing, but it was difficult for me being on the other side having to send designers home.*

# 4

## BECOMING JENÉ

### Beginning The Transition

I entered therapy during this time. Indashio, true to form, would not die without putting up a fight; I felt like I had at least three personalities inside me, vying for supremacy. On top of that, there was the stress of transitioning—hormones, electrolysis, legally changing my name and gender—and, of course, my unaddressed childhood trauma. I was overwhelmed.

Though I didn't love therapy—I never fully warmed up to my first therapist, who was always berating me for being late—it opened up a kind of necessary emotional portal. One day, I was feeling particularly tender as I left my therapist's office, and I got a call from my mom. "Hi Mom," I said. "I'm just leaving therapy." "I have something to tell you," she said. "Aunt Judy died." I immediately burst into tears. "I have something to tell you too," I said. "I'm trans!" After a moment of silence, my mother said "Maybe you shouldn't go to therapy if it makes you this upset."

Coming out to my family would be a journey, for sure—but at least I had finally broken the seal.

My family didn't know what to do with my new identity. In a way, they had to transition too. They had to mourn their son, brother, nephew, and grandson. I knew that there never really had been a Brad, that the person they'd known as "Brad" had been little more than a façade. But to them, he had been real, and they had to grieve him as though he'd died.

My mother finally got the picture when I said, "Would you rather have Jené, or would you rather have a dead child? Because it's that serious." After that, she worked harder to use my name and honor my pronouns.

My family's reaction, overall, was mixed. On the one hand, my cousins and aunts immediately hopped onboard, correcting anyone who misgendered me: "It's she, SHE." They were very protective. I wore a dress to my sister's bridal shower, and my grandma even started buying me dresses.

But there were limits. Before my sister's wedding, my grandma called me and said, "I don't think you should wear a dress, wear a suit to the wedding. She wants her brother there." That really broke my heart. I complied and wore the suit, because I didn't want to upset my sister on her special day, but I told her and my grandma afterward how hurtful an ask this had been. I felt, once again, like my family didn't see me, like they thought I was inherently wrong, like I couldn't be myself or that my existence and identity would embarrass or shame them.

I know I'm very lucky, compared to many trans people who aren't accepted by their families at all, are kicked out or shunned. My family, despite their flaws, are ultimately loving and supportive. But the sting of every rejection, every request to obscure who I was for the sake of others' comfort, has stayed with me. There's a reason that trans people face both murder and suicide at higher-than-usual rates.

I dream now of becoming a mother to young queer or trans kids—of giving them the kind of acceptance and support that I never received as a child. I also feel a responsibility to create a positive voice and image for trans people. In the last few years, we have become more visible, largely through the platforms of famous trans women like Caitlyn Jenner and Laverne Cox (a national treasure, as far as I'm concerned). It's heartening to see trans actresses like Trace Lyssette getting more roles; increasingly, trans people are portrayed as complex human beings, not tragic or hypersexualized stereotypes. Documentaries like "Disclosure" draw attention to the portrayals of trans people in the media. These days, everyone is talking about pronouns, and bathrooms are changing their signage to become more gender-inclusive. It's encouraging to see these changes, but there's so much work left to do, and I want to contribute.

THIS LITTLE LIGHT OF MINE

# Jené Emerges

During this time, the name "Jené Sais Quoi" started popping into my head. Though it didn't stick at first with my friends and family—at this point my friends called me Dasha (a feminization of Indashio), and my mom called me Tippy—the name just wouldn't leave me alone. It just fit. Over time, I began to think of myself as Jené, and to introduce myself that way. The name, like INDASHIO, chose me.

Finally, I got to be my own muse. Rather than dressing up my sister, or my friends, or professional models, I could focus on myself. I began painting, and became absorbed in completing a series of self-portraits. My friends teased me for my self-obsession; I took it good-naturedly. I knew that this in fact wasn't ego—the kind of superiority complex with which Indashio was afflicted—but rather self-love. For the first time in my life, I was falling in love with who I really was. I'd dress myself in the morning like I was my own fashion show, and the world was my runway. I became my own living art.

I began reinventing myself, exploring new forms of self-expression. I made art, I wrote, I danced, I dreamed of acting. I enrolled in community college, finally ready to get my degree, to have the college experience I'd circumvented in my quest for riches and fame. I studied art, screenwriting, acting, and business. I love being a student, having the time and space and support to experiment with new forms of knowledge and creativity, while making new friends from a place of true authenticity.

One day, contemplating my newfound dream of acting, I asked the universe for a sign. The universe was prompt: that very day, I got a text from a casting director. They were looking for a fashion designer to appear in a film that a major studio was about to start shooting. I didn't have to think twice—I was in.

I arrived on set on cloud nine. My good mood was boosted when the stylist complimented my outfit. But then, my heart sank when I was directed to the dressing room—the men's dressing room. I asked politely if I could use the women's room. (At this point I had been on hormones for almost a year and was fully out). They told me no and sent me, again, to the men's room. There, I got strange looks and more than one "are you in the right place, lady?" It was so uncomfortable changing in front of men again—like being in the Pittsfield high school gym locker room all over again.

The next day, I didn't go back. When they called to ask where I was, I told them that I wasn't coming back if I'd have to use the men's dressing room. They agreed to create a separate space for me to change in, which turned out to be just a small section of hallway.

I ended up hiring an attorney and suing the studio. My case was pretty clear: under state law, they were required to provide me with a space that aligned with my gender identity, and they'd failed to do this. We settled the case, but the best part was that the studio, having recognized their mistake, flew me out to LA and invited me to consult with them about how they could do better in the future. It was a nice silver lining—knowing that my feedback would help prevent other trans and nonbinary people from having similar experiences in the future. With the money from the settlement, I was also finally able to get my own apartment.

I'm finally back on my feet, but I'm trying not to rush anything. Having finally become Jené, I'm taking time to figure out who Jené is and how she wants to express herself in the world.

What I'm learning is that, in many ways, Jené is the opposite of Indashio. She's very private, and loves to spend time alone. She can be very expressive, but she can also be reserved. She doesn't drink or do drugs.

Looking back, when I think of Brad and Indashio, I see them as friends; they knew how hard it would be for Jené to exist in this world, and they protected her until she was ready to emerge. Living within those personas allowed me to survive until I knew who I really was.

I think often of those I hurt along the way in my journey. It's true what they say, that "hurt people hurt people." For so long I was trapped, yearning to escape, and in my pain I often lashed out at others, or used them to get ahead. When I think of this, I am sorry from the bottom of my heart. I have learned to forgive myself, to have compassion for the suffering person who sometimes acted like a self-centered asshole; I can see now how I was just looking for myself, and how everything I needed was inside me the whole time. I am now able to give myself the love and acceptance I was yearning for all of those years. I feel the same compassion for those who have hurt me. Everyone just wants to be loved and accepted. We all make mistakes and hurt others along the way, and we all deserve compassion.

There is so much more for me to discover about who I really am, and how to use my voice. I am still figuring out my next steps. Though I have ideas—about film projects I'd like to do, and a line of organic wellness products; about becoming a movie star or business mogul—I'm mostly being patient and waiting to see what the universe has in store for me. I still dream about someday owning a brownstone in New York that becomes a home to queer kid runways with no place else to go; I dream of becoming a mother and mentor to younger people who struggle the same way I did. But for now, Jené is still a kid herself; I want to let her have her youth.

Out of all my dreams, the biggest one has already come true: the dream of fully being myself. I hope that my story will inspire others to honor their own "inner light" and find ways to let it shine unapologetically upon the world.

THIS LITTLE LIGHT OF MINE

*My best friend Eva captured this photo. It was amazing to see my beauty for the first time Miami 2016*

THIS LITTLE LIGHT OF MINE

*My wardrobe fitting for my first movie & what I wore while having to change in front of men on set in 2016*

*JSQ original 2017. After watching the movie "The Danish Girl,"
I was inspired to paint my transition and become my own muse*

*In front of my art in my Manhattan apartment, wearing one of my designs and being my own muse.
I love this girl!*

# THIS LITTLE LIGHT OF MINE

*Jené at New York Fashion Week in 2018. My Le Ne Je Ne "Gone with The Wind" inspired collection*

THIS LITTLE LIGHT OF MINE

*Jené's first fashion shoot in 2016 by Rafael Fuchs. Make up by Natasha*

THIS LITTLE LIGHT OF MINE

*Happiness, playing dress up and making art. Miami 2017*

*Jené's debut at NYFW 2017 the show was one of my most artist moments
& also like a funeral & birth*

### THIS LITTLE LIGHT OF MINE

*It felt great to finally see the girl I was in the mirror. I am so proud and love the person I have become. Brave! NYC 2017*

*The butterfly emerges & now she soars. Experiencing the magic of life & the universe. Bali 2020*

www.ingramcontent.com/pod-product-compliance
Lightning Source LLC
Chambersburg PA
CBHW042027050526
44107CB00103B/722